MIDJOURNEY DIGEST

List of Words

1000+ words to add to your prompts

+ Prompt Ideas

Make AI Art That Sells

By Milena Sladkova

Content:

Scan the code to join our newly created Facebook Group. You can post your AI-generated content, share your products, and ask for opinions from other members. We are going to discuss ways _how to turn your AI art into profit_. Ask for help if you need it.

See you there!

Introduction

Midjourney is a revolutionary platform that has made creating art accessible and easy for artists of all levels. This innovative tool uses cutting-edge AI algorithms to help artists generate stunning and unique pieces of art with just a few clicks. With its user-friendly interface and intuitive design, Midjourney has simplified the art-making process, making it accessible to everyone, even those who don't have a background in art. Midjourney offers an impressive array of features, including the ability to customize your artwork with a range of parameters and settings, making it easy to create stunning and highly personalized pieces of art. Whether you're a professional artist looking to explore new creative avenues or a hobbyist looking to try your hand at art-making, Midjourney offers a fun and exciting way to create art.

What is important to know?

Once you access the servers of Midjourney you have 25 free images which you can generate in "newbies" channels. Head to any of the channels type **/imagine** and continue writing your prompt. Midjourney has been trained to generate AI Art using trillions of images. The results are mostly stunning. What is important to know is that *you are not allowed to use the 25 free images with commercial purposes*. This means you can only use them to try out the tool. If you want to use the images with commercial purposes, *you will need to buy a subscription*. The subscription can be purchased monthly or yearly. Before you purchase a plan, make sure you know why you want to use Midjourney and therefore which plan is going to be best suitable for you.

Here is how much Midjourney costs:

Source: www.midjourney.com

Plan Comparison

	Free Trial	Basic Plan	Standard Plan	Pro Plan
Monthly Subscription Cost	-	$10	$30	$60
Annual Subscription Cost	-	$96 ($8 / month)	$288 ($24 / month)	$576 ($48 / month)
Fast GPU Time	0.4 hr/lifetime	3.3 hr/month	15 hr/month	30 hr/month
Relax GPU Time Per Month	-	-	Unlimited	Unlimited
Purchase Extra GPU Time	-	$4/hr	$4/hr	$4/hr
Work Solo In Your Direct Messages	-	✓	✓	✓

	Free Trial	Basic Plan	Standard Plan	Pro Plan
Stealth Mode	-	-	-	✓
Maximum Queue	3 concurrent Jobs 10 Jobs waiting in queue	3 concurrent Jobs 10 Jobs waiting in queue	3 concurrent Jobs 10 Jobs waiting in queue	12 concurrent Fast Jobs 3 concurrent Relaxed Jobs 10 Jobs waiting in queue
Rate Images to Earn Free GPU Time	-	✓	✓	✓
Usage Rights	CC BY-NC 4.0	General Commercial Terms*	General Commercial Terms*	General Commercial Terms*

- If you have subscribed at any point, you are free to use your images in just about any way you want. If you are a company making more than $1,000,000 USD in gross revenue per year, you must purchase the Pro plan.

For any additional information head to the Midjourney website:

https://docs.midjourney.com/

Controversy and ethical issues

Using the names of Artists:

This book contains a list of the names of different artists. Using the name (or names) of one or more artists in your prompt results in this, that the generated images resembling the style of the artist. Artists are in general not happy that AI has used their artwork to train their algorithms. You can try how your art will turn out if you add the names of your favourite artists to your prompt, but if you are planning on using this art for *commercial purposes* it is definitely *not* recommended to do so. Maybe a much safer idea is to use the style, or a mix of styles because anyone can create in that particular style without the potential of a lawsuit.

Here is a simple example of why you should not use a name of an artist. One of the ways to make money out of your AI Art is to sell it stock images. There are many websites where people sell their stock images, but there are not many that accept AI-generated images. For example, one of the biggest websites for stock photos Shutterstock has banned AI-generated images (information actual as of 02/2023). Luckily for AI creators another big website *Adobe Stock* accepts AI-generated images. There are many requirements that one should have in mind before generating anything.

1. You cannot upload an image which represents a real person. This means you cannot create your art using the names of your favourite actors or your favourite comic figures.

2. If you create any fictional person you have to submit a property release for that person.

3. You need to write the whole prompt you used to create your image in the description.

4. Very important: you cannot have a name of another artist in your prompt, otherwise your images won't be accepted and your account may even get banned.

That's why it is quite important to be aware of the legal side of creating AI Art. This is not any legal advice, just an informative text.

If you are planning to upload content to sites like Adobe Stock, make sure you familiarise yourself with all the guidelines, to make sure you have a higher chance of your images being accepted.

Tipp: Any content uploaded on Adobe Stock, cannot be uploaded to other websites.

Ideas of images to generate

There are many ways to sell your art. In this book, we will concentrate on selling your images on stock websites. As mentioned before Adobe Stock is one of the biggest websites that accepts AI-generated images. Here are a few ideas and trending topics that could sell well as a stock image. It's important to explore the topic, make a research what already exists and create your prompt so that you get stunning and most importantly useful results:

~ ~ ~

1. **"Neural Dreamscapes"**: Use neural network techniques to generate surreal landscapes and dreamlike scenes that can be used as backgrounds for designs and layouts.

- "Ethereal landscapes": Generate dreamlike landscapes that depict an otherworldly and ethereal atmosphere, featuring soft colors and flowing shapes.
- "Surreal cityscapes": Create surreal and abstract cityscapes that depict a twisted and fantastical version of urban environments, featuring distorted buildings and unexpected elements.
- "Alien worlds": Generate landscapes that depict strange and mysterious alien worlds, featuring unusual flora and fauna, and unearthly atmospheric conditions.
- "Post-apocalyptic environments": Create landscapes that depict the aftermath of a catastrophic event, featuring ruined cities, overgrown wilderness, and a sense of desolation and abandonment.
- "Psychedelic realms": Generate landscapes that depict a trippy and otherworldly realm, featuring bright colors, unexpected shapes, and a sense of disorientation and wonder.

~ ~ ~

2. **"Generative Portraits"**: Use AI to generate unique and abstract portrait art that can be used in a wide range of contexts, such as in book covers, posters, and websites.

- "Futuristic avatars": Create portraits of futuristic avatars or digital beings that depict a sense of advanced technology and artificial intelligence.
- "Surreal self-portraits": Generate surreal and abstract self-portraits that depict a twisted and fantastical version of the self, featuring distorted features and unexpected elements.

- "Ethereal faces": Create portraits that depict ethereal and otherworldly beings, featuring soft colors and flowing shapes.
- "Alien entities": Generate portraits that depict strange and mysterious alien entities, featuring unusual features and unearthly expressions.
- "Post-human forms": Create portraits that depict post-human forms, featuring a mix of organic and mechanical elements, and a sense of evolution and transcendence.

~ ~ ~

3. **"Fractal Abstractions"**: Create generative art using fractal algorithms that can be used as backgrounds or elements in designs and layouts.

- "Cosmic fractals": Generate fractal abstractions that depict a cosmic or outer space theme, featuring bright colors, swirling patterns, and a sense of infinity and wonder.
- "Fractal landscapes": Create abstract fractal landscapes that depict a mix of natural and artificial elements, featuring intricate patterns and a sense of depth and movement.
- "Neo-futurist fractals": Generate fractal abstractions that depict a neo-futurist theme, featuring geometric shapes, bold colors, and a sense of technology and progress.
- "Organic fractals": Create fractal abstractions that depict organic forms, featuring flowing shapes, natural colors, and a sense of growth and movement.
- "Psychedelic fractals": Generate fractal abstractions that depict a trippy and otherworldly realm, featuring bright colors, unexpected shapes, and a sense of disorientation and wonder.

~ ~ ~

4. **"AI-generated typography"**: Create unique and abstract lettering and typography using AI techniques, which can be used in a variety of contexts, such as in book covers, posters, and websites.

- "Neon typography": Generate typography that features neon colors and a futuristic, technological theme.
- "Surreal letters": Create typography that features distorted or abstract letterforms and unexpected elements, evoking a sense of the surreal.
- "Ethereal typography": Generate typography that features soft colors and flowing shapes, evoking a sense of otherworldliness and ethereal.
- "Alien script": Create typography that features unusual letterforms and symbols, evoking a sense of alien or extraterrestrial origin.
- "Post-apocalyptic typography": Generate typography that features distressed, eroded, or abandoned elements, evoking a sense of desolation and abandonment.

~ ~ ~

5. **"Neural-style transfer"**: Use neural style transfer techniques to create new artworks by merging the styles of different images, such as combining the style of a painting with a photograph.

- "Surreal masterpieces": Generate new images by applying neural-style transfer techniques to well-known masterpieces, creating surreal and fantastical versions of the original works.
- "Ethereal landscapes": Create new images by applying neural-style transfer techniques to photographs of natural landscapes, creating ethereal and otherworldly versions of the original images.

- "Futuristic cities": Generate new images by applying neural-style transfer techniques to photographs of urban environments, creating a futuristic and technologically advanced version of the original image.
- "Alien worlds": Create new images by applying neural-style transfer techniques to photographs of natural landscapes, creating strange and mysterious alien worlds.
- "Psychedelic art": Generate new images by applying neural-style transfer techniques to photographs of natural landscapes, creating trippy and otherworldly version of the original images with bright colors and unexpected shapes.

~ ~ ~

6. **"AI-generated patterns"**: Create intricate and unique patterns using AI techniques, which can be used as backgrounds or elements in designs and layouts.

- "Futuristic patterns": Generate patterns that feature a futuristic theme, with geometric shapes and bold colors, evoking a sense of technology and progress.
- "Organic patterns": Create patterns that feature organic shapes and natural colors, evoking a sense of growth and movement.
- "Abstract patterns": Generate patterns that are abstract and non-representational, featuring unexpected shapes and bold colors.
- "Art-deco patterns": Create patterns that feature art-deco motifs, featuring geometric shapes and bold colors, evoking a sense of nostalgia and vintage.
- "Neon patterns": Generate patterns that feature neon colors and unexpected shapes, evoking a sense of energy and innovation.

List of words

Here we are coming to the last chapter of this book. This chapter contains a lot of words that can be used in your prompts. Use them to make better prompts and generate amazing art. You know, the puppet is as good as its master. Make the most of the AI tool that you are using. You can mix styles, lighting types, materials, etc. "The sky is the limit" as some would say. Happy creating and stay tuned for more info!

Source: https://github.com/willwulfken/MidJourney-Styles-and-Keywords-Reference/tree/main/Pages/MJ_V3/Style_Pages/Just_The_Style

CAMERA

Camera, Film, and Lenses

> ### Camera and Scenes

Scene		
Photography	Photograph	Closed composition
Filmic	Cinematic	
Dramatic	Glamor Shot	
Golden Hour	Blue Hour	
Award Winning Photography	Establishing Shot	Nightography
Photoshoot	Portrait	Cinematic Haze
Subject		
Pose	Gesture	Profile
High-Speed Photograph	Time-Lapse	Motion Capture
Claymation	Video Frame Capture	
Stop Motion	Stop-motion Animation Frame	
Color Grading	Bokeh	Film Grain
Surveillance	Surveillance Footage	
Security Footage	CCTV	
Dashcam-Footage	Satellite Imagery	Paparazzi Photography
Underwater Photography	Wildlife Photography	National Geographic Photo
Editorial Photography	Associated Press Photo	Photojournalism
Action Scene	War Photography	

> ### Camera and Film Types

Camcorder Effect	DSLR	Night Vision
Drone Photography	GoPro Video	UnregisteredHypercam2
Hyperspectral Imaging	Multispectral Imaging	Schlieren
Disposable Camera	Disposable Camera Photo	
Polaroid		

Ektachrome
Kodak Ektar
Nikon D750
Lomo
Tri-X 400 TX
VistaVision
Techniscope
Panavision
Cinerama
Daguerrotype
Tintype
Full Frame

Fujifilm Superia Instax
Kodak Gold 200 Kodak Portra
Provia   Velvia
Pinhole Photography   CinemaScope
Ilford HP5   Photogram
Technirama
Super-35
Super-Panavision-70
Kinopanorama   Cinemiracle
Ambrotype   Calotype
Film-Negative

> ### Film Sizes

Shot on 8mm
Shot on 16mm
Shot on 35mm
Shot on 65mm
Shot on 70mm

Shot on 9.5mm
Shot on 17.5mm   Shot on 28mm
35mm   Expired 35mm Film
Expired 65mm Film
Shot on IMAX 70mm

> ### Lens Sizes

15mm Lens
100mm Lens

35mm Lens   85mm Lens
200mm Lens

> ### Lenses

Macro
100x Magnification
500x Magnification
Microscopic

Telescope
Telephoto
Wide Angle
Fisheye Lens

Macro View   Magnification
200x Magnification
1000x Magnification
Electron Microscope   Super-Resolution
                                     Microscopy
Telescopic   Telescope Photography
Panorama   360 Panorama
Ultra-Wide Angle   360 Angle
Fisheye Lens Effect   Lens Distortion

➤ Lens Filters

Color-Gel	Filter
Photographic-Filter	Diffusion-Filter
Dichroic-Filter	UV-Filter
Polarization-Filter	Polarizer
Infrared-Filter	Infrared-Cut-Off-Filter
Neutral-Density-Filter	ND-Filter
GND-Filter	Graduated-Neutral-Density-Filter
Astronomical-Filter	Cokin-Filter

➤ Camera Settings (Aperture, Exposure, Color and White Balance, etc.)

Exposure	Short Exposure	Long Exposure
Double-Exposure	Shutter Speed 1/1000	Shutter Speed 1/2
Aperture	F/2.8	F/22
Gamma	White Balance	

➤ Depth of Field, Zoom, Pan, and Tilt

Depth	Depth of Field	DOF
Zoom	Dolly Zoom	
Horizon Line	Vantage Point	Vanishing Point
Pan	Tilt	
Focal Point	Soft-Focus	

➤ Megapixel Resolutions

Megapixel	2 Megapixels	
10 Megapixels	12 Megapixels	16 Megapixels
20 Megapixels	22 Megapixels	

➤ Other

Lens Flare	Vignette	Split Toning
Rephotography	Scanography	Slit-Scan Photography

COLORS & PALETTES

- ➢ Colors

- o Basic Colors

White	Black	Brown
Light-Gray	Gray	Dark-Gray
Maroon	Red	Orange
Yellow	Lime	Green
Cyan	Teal	Blue
Indigo	Purple	Violet
Fuchsia	Magenta	Pink

- o Extended Colors

Tan	Beige	
Blush	Scarlet	
Olive-Green	Chartreuse	
Turquoise	Aqua	Azure

- o Dark Variations

Dark-White	Dark-Brown	
Dark-Maroon	Dark-Red	Dark-Orange
Dark-Yellow	Dark-Lime	Dark-Green
Dark-Cyan	Dark-Blue	
Dark-Purple	Dark-Magenta	Dark-Pink

- o Light Variations

Light-Black	Light-Brown	
Light-Maroon	Light-Red	Light-Orange
Light-Yellow	Light-Lime	Light-Green
Light-Cyan	Light-Blue	
Light-Purple	Light-Magenta	Light-Pink

- o Vivid Variations

Vivid-Brown	Vivid-Maroon	Vivid-Red
Vivid-Orange	Vivid-Yellow	Vivid-Lime

Vivid-Green   Vivid-Cyan   Vivid-Blue
Vivid-Purple   Vivid-Magenta   Vivid-Pink

> ## Color Based Designs

Color   Colorized   Color Wheel
Hue   Tone   Value
Gradient   Vibrance   Vivid
Spectrum   Pigment   Variegated
Pure   Purity
Faded Colors   Faded
Autochrome   EnChroma

> ## Chromatic Palettes

Palette   Color Palette
Warm Color Palette   Cool Color Palette Inverted Colors
Colorful   Multicolored   Rainbow
Spectral Color
Vibrant
Chroma   Dichromatism   Tetrachromacy
Saturated   High Saturation   Low Saturation
Neon   Electric Colors
Complimentary-Colors Supplementary-   Split-Complementary-
                     Colors   Colors

Analogous-Colors   Triadic-Colors   Tetradic-Colors
Polychromatic-Colors Tonal Colors
Light   Light Mode
Dark   Dark Mode
Tones of Black   Tones of Black   Light Blue Background
                     in Background

Light Blue Foreground

> ## Monochromatic Palettes

Monochromatic   Monochrome   Black and White
Desaturated   Sepia
Cyanopsia

> ## Contrast

Contrast
High Contrast   Low Contrast

➢ Color Models

Color Model

RGB	scRGB	CMYK
HSV	HSL	HCL
VGA	EGA	CGA
HDR	sRGB	DCI-P3
Adobe RGB	ProPhoto RGB	Pantone
YCbCr	YPbPr	Coloroid

➢ Color Motion Picture Film Systems

Technicolor	Kinemacolor	
Kodachrome	Cinecolor	Agfacolor

COMBINATIONS

Glowing Opal Pearlescent	Vibrant Opal Pearlescent
Glowing Amethyst Pearlescent	Vibrant Amethyst Pearlescent
Glowing Sapphire Pearlescent	Vibrant Sapphire Pearlescent
Glowing Emerald Pearlescent	Vibrant Emerald Pearlescent
Glowing Ruby Pearlescent	Vibrant Ruby Pearlescent
Glowing Fluorite Pearlescent	Vibrant Fluorite Pearlescent
Glowing Citrine Pearlescent	Vibrant Citrine Pearlescent
Glowing Quartz Pearlescent	Vibrant Quartz Pearlescent

Octane Render, 4k, Hyperrealistic
Dreamlike, Realistic
Colorful, Sci-Fi, Otherworldly, Realistic
Ultrarealistic, Photorealistic, Octane Render, 8k, Intricate Detail
Synesthesia, Otherworldly, Mystical

DESIGN STYLES

> Simplicity/Complexity

Simple	Simplicity	Basic
Details	Detailed	Hyperdetailed
Ornate		
Complex	Complexity	Multiplex
Kolmogorov Complexity	Cluttered	Greeble
Chaotic	Confusing	Incoherent
Intricate	Surface Detail	Intricate Surface Detail
Minimalist	Maximalist	Intricate Maximalism
Flat	Flat Design	Ukiyo-e Flat Design
Flat Shading		

> Patterns

Patterns	Polka Dot	Pinstripe
Grid	Axis Lines	Checkerboard
Halftone		
Camouflage	Damask Patterns	Memphis Pattern
Parametric Patterns	Diffraction Patterns	Voronoi
Zebra Pattern Tiger Pattern	Cow Pattern	
Rorschach		

> Elegance, Beauty, and Appeal

Elegant	Elegance	
Beauty	Beautiful	
Appeal	Marvelous	
Luxury	Luxurious	Luxe
Low-Quality	Medium-Quality	
High-Quality	Ultra-Quality	Ultra Quality
Perfection		

> Charts and Diagrams

Chart	Graph	Diagram
Ideogram	Pictogram	Phase-Space

Feynman Diagram	Map	Schematic

> Decade Styles

Feynman Diagram	Map	Schematic
20s	20s Pattern	1920s Decor
30s	30s Pattern	1930s Decor
40s	40s Pattern	1940s Decor
50s	50s Pattern	1950s Decor
60s	60s Pattern	1960s Decor
70s	70s Pattern	1970s Decor
80s	80s Pattern	1980s Decor
90s	90s Pattern	1990s Decor
Y2K Design	Y2K Pattern	
2000s Pattern	2000s Decor	
2010s Decor	2020s Decor	
1100s	1200s	1300s
1400s	1500s	1600s
1700s	1800s	1900s
1950s	1960s	1970s
1980s	1990s	2000s
2010s	2020s	3000s
4000s	5000s	

> Morphism (Skeuomorphism, Glassmorphism, etc.)

Morphism	
Skeuomorphism	Neumorphism
Neomorphism	
Glassmorphism	Claymorphism

> Cubism

Cubism	Synthetic Cubism	Mechanistic Cubism
Proto-Cubism	Cubo-Futurism	

> Expressionism

Expressionism	Cubo-Expressionism
Figurative Expressionism	Abstract Expressionism

> Neo

Neo

Neo-Baroque	Neo-Byzantine	Neo-Rococo
Neoclassicism	Neoplasticism	
Neo-Dada	Neo-Futurism	NeoSon
Neo-Tokyo	Neo-Concretism	Neo-Impressionism

> Psychedelic, Divine, Fractal, and Noise

Psychedelic	Psychedelia	Psychedelica
Psychedelic Design	Trippy	Acidwave
LSD	DMT	
Kaleidoscope	Teleidoscope	
Spirograph	Mandala	
Hippie	Hyperbolic	
Flower of Life	Sacred Geometry	
Chakra Aura	Quantum	
Divine	Ineffable	Sacred
Transcendent	Transcendental	Astral
Soul	Karma	
Fractal	Fractal Art	Fractal Environment
Mandelbrot	Multibrot	
Mandelbox	Mandelbulb	
Julia-Set	Lyapunov-Fractal	Burning-Ship-Fractal
Newton Fractal	Newton-Fractal	
Noisy	Noise	White Noise
Cell Noise	Perlin Noise	Simplex Noise

> Synesthesia

Synesthesia	Synesthetic
Chromesthesia	
Music-Color Synesthesia	Musical-Color Synesthesia
Music-Vision Synesthesia	Musical-Texture Synesthesia
Chords-Color Synesthesia	Musical-Spatial Synesthesia
Music-Number Synesthesia	Music-Temperature Synesthesia
Music-Smell Synesthesia	Music-Taste Synesthesia
Auditory-Visual Synesthesia	Auditory-Tactile Synesthesia
Auditory-Gustatory Synesthesia	Sound-Texture Synesthesia
Sound-Tactile Synesthesia	Sound-Touch Synesthesia
Sound-Shape Synesthesia	Sound-Number Synesthesia
Sound-Kinetics Synesthesia	Sound-Temperature Synesthesia
Sound-Smell Synesthesia	Sound-Taste Synesthesia

Aura Synesthesia
Emotion-Color Synesthesia
Concepts-Shape Synesthesia
Concept-Smell Synesthesia

Spatial-Sequence Synesthesia
Gustatory-Visual Synesthesia
Gustatory-Tactile Synesthesia
Kinetics-Color Synesthesia
Grapheme-Texture Synesthesia
Grapheme-Color Synesthesia
Grapheme-Temperature Synesthesia
Grapheme-Taste Synesthesia
Lexeme-Taste Synesthesia
Lexeme-Motor Synesthesia
Morpheme-Color Synesthesia
Letter-Color Synesthesia
Letter-Texture Synesthesia
Letter-Personality Synesthesia
Letter-Taste Synesthesia
Letter-Spatial Location Synesthesia

Personality-Color Synesthesia
Concepts-Color Synesthesia
Concept-Sound Synesthesia
Mathematical Concepts-Visual Synesthesia
Number-Form Synesthesia
Gustatory-Auditory Synesthesia
Olfactory-Visual Synesthesia
Grapheme-Shape Synesthesia
Grapheme-Image Synesthesia
Grapheme-Sound Synesthesia
Grapheme-Smell Synesthesia
Lexeme-Olfactory Synesthesia
Lexical-Gustatory Synesthesia
Lexeme-Color Synesthesia
Words-Color Synesthesia
Letter-Shape Synesthesia
Letter-Image Synesthesia
Letter-Smell Synesthesia
Letter-Sound Synesthesia
Letter-Temperature Synesthesia

> Art Styles

Pop-Art	Warhol	Fauvism
Lo-fi	Hi-fi	High Fidelity
Biomorphic	Ornamental	
Bauhaus Style	Modernism	Composition
Transautomatism	Cloisonnism	Orphism
Suprematism	Vorticism	Eccentrism
Rayonism	Spectralism	Luminism
Muralism	Spatialism	Diptych
Precisionism	Regionalism	
Classical	Classicism	Academicism
Miserablism	Synchronism	Romanticism
Constructivist	Constructivism	
Baroque	Rococo	Positivism
Pictorialism	Gothic	
Tubism	Naturalism	Idyllic
Vedute	Verism	Divisionism
Nuagisme	Sumatraism	Anachronism
Synthetism	Tonalism	Barbouillage
Orientalism	Symbolism	Lettrism

Biedermeier
Idealism
Impressionism
Art Deco
Award Winning Art
Folk Art
Renaissance
Lowbrow
Dada
Medievalism
Multidimensional Art
Fourier Art
Anti
Compound Design
Tactile Design
Tachisme
Frasurbane
Triptych
Silhouette
Incoherents
Store-Brand
Amate
Brocade
Escapism
Existentialism

Purism
Post-Impressionism
Art Nouveau
Epic Composition
Postcolonial Art
Harlem-Renaissance
Figurativism
Dadaism
New Medievalism
Temporary Art
Nebulous Art
Anti-Design
Grunge Revival
Memphis Style
Avant-Garde
Sfumato
Foreshortening
Topographic
Existential
Contemporary
Wuhtercuhler

Ligne Claire
Lovecraftian

Intimism
Dau al Set
Nouveau Realisme
Drop Art

Neo-Dadaism
Vienna Secession
Op Art
Mozarabic Art

Design Stuckism
Memphis Design
Transavantgarde
Neue Sachlichkeit
Booru
Chiaroscuro
Kitsch
Costumbrismo

Bohemianism

> Stylized

Design
Combine
Layered
Bubble Design

Bling
Lissajous
Alignment
Droste Effect
Molecular
Shockwave
Oddly Satisfying
Zygomorphic

Style
Combination
Photobash
Extreme Bubble Design
Jewel Tones
Patched
Misalignment
Stabilimentum
Qubit
Edge-To-Edge

Stylized
Seamless
Cut
Liquify

Blocky

Compression
Precision

> ## Other Styles

Generic		
Balance	Proportion	Blending
Representation		
Lossy	Rodilius	
Kerkythea	Mottled	
Qbist	Oilify	
Entropy	Zalgo	Liminal
Crooked	Cockeyed	
Extreme	Elite	
Artifact		
Serendipity	Acidic	
Oudemansiella-Mucida	Podoserpula-Miranda	
Gliophorus-Psittacinus		
Tint	Shade	

DIGITAL

> ## Rendering Engines

Rendering Engine		
Octane	Cinema4D	C4D
Unreal Engine	Unity Engine	
Rendered in Houdini	Houdini-Render	Redshift Render
Blender Render	Cycles Render	OptiX-Render
Povray	Vray	CryEngine
LuxCoreRender	Silicon Render	
MentalRay-Render	Raylectron	
Infini-D-Render	Zbrush	Sketchfab
OpenGL	DirectX	
Autodesk 3ds Max	SketchUp	Terragen
Arnold Render		

> ## Resolution

4k	8k	16k
32k	Super-Resolution	
UHD	Ultra-HD	

HD	Full-HD	
144p	240p	480p
720p	1080p	

> Aspect Ratios and Letterboxing

Fullscreen	Widescreen	Anamorphic Widescreen
Pillarbox	Letterboxing	Windowbox

> 1-bit - 16-bit

1-bit	2-bit	3-bit
4-bit	4-bit RGB	6-bit
8-bit	8-bit RGB	
12-bit	12-bit RGB	
16-bit	16-bit RGB	

> Digital Styles

AR	VR	HQ
Virtualcore	Technocore	
Cyberspace	Cyberdelic	
Cyberprep	Cybernoir	Cybernetics
Hexatron	Trillwave	
Analog	Analogpunk	
Digital	Digitalpunk	
Cyber Minimalism	Frutiger Aero	Abstract Tech
Emulated	Pixelscape	
Memecore	Old Memecore	
Old Web		
Algorithmic		

> VFX and Video Companies

Disney	Pixar	Dreamworks
IMAX	Imageworks	Framestore
Pixomondo	Luma Pictures	Criterion Collection

> Art Programs and Applications

Program	App	Application
Microsoft Paint	MSPaint	Drawn in Kid Pix

Photoshop   Adobe Lightroom   Drawn in Illustrator
Adobe Premier   After Effects
Adobe Flash   Shockwave Flashplayer
Drawn in Paint.NET   Drawn in GIMP
Drawn in Photo-Paint-X5
Drawn in Aseprite   Drawn in Pyxel Edit

> ## Image Formats and Types

Graphic   Graphics
Picture   Image
Raster   Vector Graphics
Bitmap   Jpeg   Icon
Animated GIF   Video
Render   Rendered   Rendering
3D Model   3D Render   Precision Rendering
Wiremap   Lowpoly   Low Poly
Pre-Rendered Graphics   Physically Based Rendering
Holographic   Holography
Texture   Seamless Texture
Digital Art   Pixel Art   Voxel Art
Pixel-Perfect   ASCII   Tilemap
Meme   NFT   Clip Art
Photomontage   Stock Photo   Wallpaper
Procedural Texture   Algorithmic Art   Character Design
Creative Commons Attribution

> ## Dithering

Dither   Dithering
Floyd–Steinberg Dithering   Bayer-Matrix Dithering
2x2-Bayer-Matrix Dithering   4x4-Bayer-Matrix Dithering
8x8-Bayer-Matrix Dithering
Burkes Dithering   Stucki Dithering   Atkinson Dithering
Jarvis-Judice-Ninke Dithering   Sierra Dithering
Gradient-Based Error-Diffusion Dithering

> ## Websites

Website   Webbrutalism   Geocities
Artstation   Polycount   Trending on Artstation
DeviantArt   Flickr   Behance

Social Media
Art on Instagram   Instagram-Art   Artstation-Art
CGSociety   Pixiv   Unsplash
Google Maps

> ➤ Glitchy

Glitchcore   Matrix
Glitchy   Glitching
Data Moshing   Datamoshing   Databending
Data Manipulation   Artifacting   Fuzzing

> ➤ AI and Neural Networks

AI   Neural Network
AI Generated   Neural Art   Neural Style Transfer
Deep Dream
Generated by Midjourney   Generated by Dall-e   Generated by Dall-e2
Convolutional Features   Image Segmentation

> ➤ Game System Graphics

Atari Graphics
Atari 2600   Atari 2600 Palette
Atari ST   Atari ST Palette
PS1 Graphics
PS2 Graphics   PS3 Graphics
PS4 Graphics   PS5 Graphics
PSP Graphics   PS Vita Graphics
Xbox Graphics   Xbox 360 Graphics
Xbox One Graphics   Xbox One X Graphics
NES   NES Palette
SNES   SNES Palette
Nintendo 64 Graphics   GameCube Graphics
Wii Graphics   Wii U Graphics
Nintendo Switch Graphics
Game Boy   Game Boy Palette   Gameboy Graphics
Game Boy Color   Game Boy Color Palette
Game Boy Advance   Game Boy Advance Palette
Nintendo DS Graphics   Nintendo 3DS Graphics

> ➤ Video Game Styles

Game   Video Game   Flash Game
HD Mod
Gamercore   Nintencore   Nintendo
Tetris   Tetris Style
Pacman   Pac-Man Style
Minecraft   Minecraft Style
Terraria   Terraria Style
Roblox
No Mans Sky
Farmville
Guitar Hero
Fallout   Fallout 4 Style
Skyrim   Skyrim Style   Morrowind Style
Stardew Valley Style Sid Meiers Civilization Style
Super Mario Style   Pokemon Style
Angry Birds Style   Candy Crush Saga Style
Polybius   LSD-Dream-Emulator
Among Us Style   The Sims 4 Style Cyberpunk 2077 Style
Fortnite Style   PUBG Style
Doom 3 Style   Quake 3 Style
Grand Theft Auto Style Forza Horizon Style
Assassins Creed Style Destiny 2 Style   Mass Effect 3 Style
Call of Duty Style   Battlefield Style
Batman Arkham Knight Style Marvels Spider-Man Style
Star Wars The Old Republic Style
Bioshock Style Resident Evil Style
Silent Hill 2 Style
Dark Souls 3 Style   Ghost of Tsushima Style
For Honor Style
The Last of Us Style   Dishonored Style Prey Style
Bloodborne Style   Disco Elysium Style
Far Cry Style   Uncharted 4 Style
DOTA 2 Style   Counter-Strike Style
League of Legends Style
Overwatch Style   Runescape Style Starcraft Style
Gears of War Style   God of War Style
Total War Warhammer Style
World of Warcraft Style Diablo Style   Fable 2 Style
Witcher Style   Witcher 3 Style   Hearthstone Style
Final Fantasy Style   Divinity Original Sin 2 Style
Dragon Age Style
Horizon Zero Dawn Style Legends of Runeterra Style
Monster Hunter Rise Style

Ori and The Blind Forest Style
The Long Dark Style
Castlevania Style   Darksiders Style   Graveyard Keeper Style
Dune Spice Wars Style   Lineage 2 Style
XCOM 2 Style   Heroes of Might and Magic 3 Style
Sea of Theaves Style
Shadowrun Style   Stray Style
FIFA 18 Style

> ## Computer System Graphics

PC Graphics
Commodore 64   Commodore 64 Palette
Commodore 128   Commodore 128 Palette
Commodore VIC-20   Commodore VIC-20 Palette
Amiga OCS Graphics   Teletext   Teletext Palette
Apple II   Apple II Palette
Apple IIGS   IIGS Graphics   Apple IIGS Palette
ZX Spectrum   ZX Spectrum Palette
Mattel Aquarius   Mattel Aquarius Palette

> ## Operating Systems

OS   Operating System
Windows-95   Windows-XP   Windows-Vista
Windows-7   Windows-8
Windows-10   Windows-11
Classic-Mac-OS   Mac-OSX   MacOS
iOS
Linux   Ubuntu

> ## Other

Network
90s Computer Graphics   1990s Computer Graphics
Cellular Automata   Conway's Game of Life
Macroblock   Photoillustration
Capcha   Recapcha

DIMENSIONALITY

➤ <u>0D-5D</u>

0-Dimensional	0-D
1-Dimensional	1-D
2-Dimensional	2D
2.5-Dimensional	2.5D
3-Dimensional	3D
4-Dimensional	4D
5-Dimensional	5D

➤ <u>Overdimensional, Multiverse, etc.</u>

Dimensionality

Overdimensional	Underdimensional	Hyperdimensional
Subdimensional	Everdimensional	Omnidimensional
Extradimensional	Beyond-Dimensional	Excessively-dimensional
Alldimensional	Multiverse	
Parallel-Universe	Perpendicular-Universe	

DRAWING AND ART MEDIUMS

➢ Illustration and Drawing
  o Drawing Types

Sketch	Drawing	Doodle
Hand-Drawn	Hand-Written	Children's Drawing
Masterpiece		
Dot Art	Pointillism	Stipple
Line Art	Crosshatch	Etch-A-Sketch Drawing
Figure Drawing	Caricature	
Illustration	Storybook Illustration	Illustrated-Booklet
Whimsical Illustration	Archaeological Illustration	
Assembly Drawing	Anatomical Drawing	Illuminated Manuscript
Visual Novel	Graphic Novel	Cartographic
Storyboard		

  o Pencil and Graphite

Pencil Art	Graphite	Charcoal Art
Colored Pencil	Grease Pencil	

➢ Ink

Ink	Calligraphy	Ballpoint Pen
Fountain Pen	Fountain Pen Art	Gel Pen
Conductive Ink	Flexographic Ink	

India Ink	Iron Gall Ink	
Grease Pen	Marker Art	
Dry-Erase Marker	Wet-Erase Marker	Whiteboard
Viscosity Print		

- o <u>Crayon, Chalk, and Pastel</u>

| Crayon Chalk | Pastel Art | |
| Blackboard | Chalkboard | Conte |

- ➤ <u>Paint</u>
- o <u>Painting Types</u>

Painting	Canvas Hard	Edge Painting
Oil Painting	Tempera Painting	Acrylic Painting
Watercolor Painting	Gouache Painting	Casein Painting
Fresco Painting	Easel Painting	Wet Painting
Detailed Painting	Speedpainting	Faux Painting
Color Field Painting	Scroll Painting	
Still Life	Still-Life	
Fine Art	Modern Art	
Brushwork	Paintwork	Impasto
Matte Painting	Encaustic Painting	Gond Painting
Chinese Painting	Romanesque Painting	Ancient Roman Painting
Tibetan Painting	Japanese Painting	
Warli Painting	Fayum Portrait	Caravaggio Painting

Madhubani Painting	Kalamkari Painting	Phad Painting
Paper-Marbling	Hydro-Dipping	Hydrodipped
Panel Painting	Sand Painting	
Plein-Air Painting	Action Painting	Miniature Painting
Artwork	Mural	Street Art
Cave Art	Rock Art	Sandpainting
Easter Egg	Egg Decorating	

o Paint Types

Paint	Oil Paint	Tempera Paint
Acrylic Paint	Gouache Paint	Watercolor
Wet Paint	Dripping Paint	Splatter Paint
Graffiti	Stencil Graffiti	Graffiti Tag
Airbrush	1980s Airbrush Art	Puffy Paint
Spray	Spray Paint	Glass Paint
Blacklight Paint	Casein Paint	Coffee Paint
Powder Paint		

➢ Text

Hypergraphy	Asemic Writing	
Text	Typeface	Font
Letters	Written Letters	Written Letters "Hello"
Written Words	Written Words "Hello"	
Words	Words "Hello"	

Lexemes	Lexemes "Hello"	Graphemes
Says	Says Hello	Says "Hello"
Says 'Hello'	Caption	Caption "Hello"

- ➢ <u>Printed Material</u>
  - o <u>Print Types</u>

Print	Printed	3D Printed
Inkjet Printed	Laser Printed	
Edge-To-Edge	Photographic Print	
Photolith Film		
Concept Art	Logo	
Album Art	Cover-Art	
Newspaper	Newsprint	
Risograph	Lithography	Flexography
Transfer Printing	Monotype	
Blueprint	Whiteprint	
Sticker	Watermark	
Barcode	QR Code	

- o <u>Block Printing</u>

Block Printing	
Bagh Print	Bagru Print

- <u>Cards and Stamps</u>

Stamp	Postage Stamp	Business Card
Pokemon Card	Pokémon Card	Tarot Card

- <u>Books and Posters</u>

Magazine	Comic Book	Underground Comix
Pop-up Book	Kids Book	
Booklet	Instruction Manual	IKEA Guide
Poster	Movie Poster	Concert Poster

- ➢ <u>Physical Mediums</u>
  - <u>Origami</u>

Origami	Rigid Origami	Modular Origami
Kirigami	Moneygami	Wet-Folding
Iris-Folding	Chinese Paper Art	Sonobe

- <u>Mosaic</u>

Mosaic	Micromosaic	Glass Mosaic
Photographic Mosaic	Impressionist Mosaic	
Pietra Dura	Encaustic Tile	
Ancient Roman Mosaic		

- <u>Framed, Banner, and Decal</u>

Frame	Framed

Wooden Frame	Wooden Framed	
Banner	Vinyl Banner	
Sign	Signage	Enamel Sign
Decal	Wall Decal	
Letter Board	Nameplate	Builder's Plate
Billboard	Placard	
SpellBrite		
Bumper Sticker	Fridge Magnet	
Tapestry	Bayeux Tapestry	In The Style of Bayeux Tapestry
Minoan Mural		

o <u>Carving, Etching, and Modeling</u>

Carving	Pyrography	Etching
Model	Modeling	
Sculpture	Mayan Sculpture	
Whittling	Woodcut	
Wood-Carving	Woodturning	
Chip-Carving	Chip-Work	
Chainsaw-Carving	Lath Art	Laser-Cut
Bentwood	Woodblock Print	Intarsia
Marquetry	Wood Marquetry	Straw Marquetry
Scrimshaw	Sgraffito	
Hardstone Carving	Leather Crafting	
Megalithic Art	Runic Carving	

Bejeweled	Engraved Gem	Lapidary
Relief-Carving	Ice-Carving	Intaglio
Drypoint	Metalcut	Photogravure
Lacquer	Carved Lacquer	
Papercutting	Paper Model	Paper-Mache
Stencil	Decoupage	
String-Art	Fretwork	Card
Mezzotint	Aquatint	Heliography
Linocut	Lino Print	
Puppet	Balloon Modelling	Balloon Twisting
Circuit	Circuitry	Computer Chip
Oshibana	Lithophane	Figurine

o Pottery and Glass

Glaze	Overglaze	
Underglaze	Inglaze	
Salt Glaze Pottery	Tin-Glazed Pottery	
Cameo Glass	Enameled Glass	Glass-Etching
Glass Blowing		
Paleolithic Pottery	Neolithic Pottery	Egyptian Faience
Tableware	Earthenware	Stoneware
Slipware	Chintzware	
Agateware	Lustreware	
Bone China	Bone Carving	

Ornament   Azulejo

- o   Scrapbooking and Collages

Collage   Photocollage   Fotocollage

Scrapbooking

- o   Light

Light Art   Light Painting   Lightpainting

Projection Mapping

- o   Other Physical Mediums

Arts and Crafts	Resin	Enamel Pin
Beadwork	Beads and String	Beads and Yarn
Tie-Dye	Confetti	
Sticker Bomb	Tattoo	
Papier-Colle	Assemblage	Featherwork
Latte Art	Coffee Stain	Smoke Art
Hedge Trimming	Site-Specific Art	Public Art
Installation Art	Land Art	
Ironwork	Carpentry	
Diorama		
Hatmaking		

➤ Other

Negative Space	Outlined	Middle Ground
Frottage		
Art Medium	Mixed Media	
Kamikiri	Indian Art	Soviet Art
Cosmorama		
Key Visual		
Braille		

EXPERIMENTAL

Here the author of the document experiments with different made-up words and sentences. If you want to be original maybe you can try using Chat GPT to help you create new and diverse sentences. Also you can try your own name and maybe the AI Tool will create a cool personal style *just for you* ☺

➤ Made-up Artists

Painted by Vincent Bob Gray   Painted by Redrick J Hubedrin

Painted by Leandrew Bengolstein

Art by Rickolas Veneyfield   Art by Gandelif Jamarison

➤ Made-up Words

Flash-Traced	Glimmer-Traced	Halometric Patterns
Lumametric	Nortonious	
Proporastable	Prospeartented	

Psychromvolucence   Shimmavolucent   Transchromacy

Origummy

> ➤ Known Made-up Words

Supercalifragilisticexpialidocious   Fiddlededee

> ➤ Garden-Path Sentences

The horse raced past the barn fell

The cotton clothing is made of grows in Mississippi

We painted the wall with cracks

The man who hunts ducks out on weekends

When Fred eats food gets thrown

Mary gave the child the dog bit a Band-Aid

The raft floated down the river sank

The complex houses married and single soldiers and their families

GEOGRAPHY & CULTURE

> ➤ Countries and Nations

Country   Nation

American-Style   American Realism

Canadian-Style   Canadian Realism

Europunk

Brazilian-Style	Brazilian Realism	
Incan	Tiwanaku	
Mexican-Style	Mexican Realism	
African-Style	African Realism	
Mali	Benin	
Australian-Style	Australian Realism	
Spanish-Style	Spanish Realism	
French-Style	French Realism	
Italian-Style	Italian Realism	
Turkish-Style	Turkish Realism	
British-Style	British Realism	
German-Style	German Realism	German Romanticism
Greek-Style	Greek Realism	Greek Icon
Greek Mythology	Greek God	Greek Goddess
Polish-Style	Polish Realism	
Hungarian-Style	Hungarian Realism	
Swiss-Style	Swiss Realism	
Swedish-Style	Swedish Realism	
Irish-Style	Irish Realism	
Roman-Style	Roman Realism	Roman Icon
Roman Mythology	Roman God	Roman Goddess
Dominican-Style	Dominican Realism	
Chinese-Style	Chinese Realism	
Tang Dynasty	Timurid	

Japanese	Taisho Period	
Japanese-Style	Japanese Realism	Japonism
Ukrainian-Style	Ukrainian Realism	
Indonesian-Style	Indonesian Realism	
Balinese	Tibetan	Khmer
Thai	Bagan	
Indian-Style	Indian Realism	
Bavarian		
Minoan	Cycladic	
Puebloan	Armenian	
Russian-Style	Russian Realism	
Propaganda	American Propaganda	Soviet Propaganda
Arabic	Caribbean	Mayan
Egyptian Art	Socialist Realism	
Nordic Mythology		
Victorian		
Byzantine	Byzantine Icon	
Christian Icon		

> Urban/Rural

Urban	Urbancore	Urban Exploration
Rural	Ruralcore	
Adventurecore	Hikecore	Prairiecore
Farmcore	Countrycore	Villagecore

| Tavernwave | Cabincore | Cottagecore |
| Hermitpunk | | |

> ## Holidays

Holiday		
Christmas	Santa	Elf
Halloween		

> ## Professions and Types of People

Boss	Master	
Police		
Warrior	Samurai	Samurai Warrior
Artist	Bard	Cleric
Clownpunk	Clowncore	
Viking	Pilgrim	
Quarterback		
Catholicpunk		
Poetcore	Scoutcore	
Kingcore	Princecore	Princesscore
Royalcore	Knightcore	
Roguecore	Villaincore	
Kidcore	Tweencore	Grandparentcore
Brocore		
John Cena		

- ➢ Fictional Non-Human Creatures

Entities

Goblin	Halfling
Warlock	Wizard
Elf	Orc
Mermaid	

- ➢ Sports

Sport	Sports	
Basketball	Baseball	Football
Soccer	Soccer Ball	
Golf	Golf Ball	
Tennis	Tennis Ball	
Hockey	Hockey Puck	
Volleyball		
Rugby	Rugby-Ball	
Skydiving		

GEOMETRY

- ➢ 2D Shapes

2D Shape	
Point	Dot

Line

Triangle	Chevron	
Square	Pentagon	
Hexagon	Hexagonal	Heptagon
Octagon	Nonagon	Decagon
Rectangle	Rectangular	Parallelogram
Rhombus	Star	Heart
Spirangle		

➤ 3D Shapes

3D Shape	Orb	
Cube	Cuboid	
Sphere	Cylinder	Torus
Pyramid	Cone	
Rectangular Prism	Star Prism	Wedge
Zonohedron	Tetrahedron	Octahedron
Dodecahedron	Icosahedron	Kepler–Poinsot Polyhedra
Cuboctahedron	Rhombicuboctahedron	Icosidodecahedron
Trapezohedron	Rhombicosidodecahedron	
Bezier Surface		
Cupola	Anticupola	Hypercupolae
Bicupola	Frustum	Bifrustum
Rotunda	Birotunda	Prismatoid
Scutoid	Bipyramid	Star Bipyramid

Antiprism	Anti-Prism	
Trapezohedra	Star Trapezohedron	Spherical Polyhedron
Mobius Strip	Hexaflexagon	Miura Fold

> ## 4D Hyper Shapes

4D Shape	Hyper Shape	4D Hyper Shape
Hyperplane	Hypersurface	
Hypercube	Tesseract	Hyperprism
Hypersphere	Hypercylinder	Hypertorus
Hyperpyramid	Hypercone	Klein Bottle
Hyperzonohedron	Hypertetrahedron	Hyperoctahedron
Hyperdodecahedron	Hypericosahedron	Flexible Polyhedron

> ## Degenerate Shapes

Monogon	Digon

> ## Geometric Styles

Geometry	Geometric	Islamic Geometric Patterns
Poly	Polygon	Polygonal
Polyhedron	Polyhedral	
Platonic Solids	Archimedean Solids	Catalan Solids
Manifold	Multifold	
Maniform	Multiform	

Non-Euclidian

Form-Constant

> Geometric Properties

Vertex	Edge	Surface
Interior	Exterior	Anterior
Convex	Concave	
Convex Hull		
Symmetry	Symmetric	Asymmetric
Equiangular	Equilateral	Cyclic
Tangential	Rectilinear	Traverse
Quasi	Quasi-Regular	
Isogonal	Isotoxal	Isohedral
Stellation	Ehrhart Polynomial	Ideal Polyhedron
Polytope		

> Topology Styles

Topology	Topological

INTANGIBLES

➤ <u>Emotions and Qualities</u>

Happy	Happy Accidents	Joyful
Excited	Euphoric	Love
Sad	Lonely	Depressing
Cheerful	Surprise	
Emotion	Emotional	
Intense	Freaky	
Clever	Brilliant	Intelligent
Whimsical		
Pleasing	Evocative	
Angry	Dangerous	
Angelic	Good	Heavenly
Evil	Diabolic	Demonic
Corrupt	Corrupted	
God	Devil	
Benevolent	Malevolent	
Troubled	Cringey	
Creepy	Horror	Frightened
Soulful	Sublime	Ideal
Luscious	Consumable	
Cute		

➢ Concepts

Concept	Conceptual	Number
Infused	Refreshing	Essence
Esoteric	Supersonic	Magnetic
Significant	Insanity	
Void		
Theme		
Neural	Bleak	Barren
Eerie	Vast	
Nothing	Something	
Anything	Everything	
Someone	Somebody	
No-one	Nobody	
Anyone	Anybody	
Forms	Freaky-Forms	
Unknown	Untitled	
Example	Instance	Incarnation
Multifarious	Diverse	
Feng Shui	Perfectionism	OCD
Knolling	Organized	Sorted
Neat	Tidy	Archive
Random	Technique	
Array	Flexible	Upside-Down
Chiral	Chirality	Ambidextrous

Continuity	Paradigm	
Representation	Manifestation	Indication
Embodiment	Quintessence	Apotheosis
Kinetic		
Muted	Silence	
Secret	Secretive	
Ambiguous Image	Bayer Matrix	
Beginning	End	Extended
Life	Death	Purgatory
Mind	Ego	Egodeath
Paradox	Cryptic	
Modified	Modification	Manipulation
Alterations		
Miscellaneous	Experimental	
Aspect	Ratio	Aspect Ratio
Physics	Wafting	
System	Prompt	
Sinusoid	Summation	
Destructive	Abrasion	
Obstructed	Convergence	
Displace	Shifted	Shifting
Accumulation	Accumulated	
Resolution	Format	
Breathing		

Play	Playing	Playful
Wulfken		
Nom	Nom-Nom	
Derp	Hurr-Durr	
Derr	Durrific	

> <u>Size</u>

Size	Bite-Sized	Scale
Nano	Micro	Tiny
Mini	Big	Large
Huge	Massive	Massive Scale

> <u>Strength and Durability</u>

Weak	Strong	Durable
Powerful		

> <u>Symbols</u>
> o <u>Zodiac Signs</u>

Capricornus	Aquarius	Pisces
Taurus	Gemini	Cancer
Leo	Virgo	Libra
Scorpio	Sagittarius	

➢ Other Symbols

Symbol	Symbols	
Emblem	Sigil	Blissymbol
Rune		
Emoticon	Emote	
Zodiac	Zodiac Sign	
Alchemical-Symbols	Astronomical-Symbols	
Logogram	Ideogram	
Lexigram	Lexigram Symbol	
Therblig	Therblig Symbol	
Glyph	Glyphigram	
Hieroglyphica	Hieroglyphical	
Yin Yang	Om Symbol	Clef
Ouroboros	Valknut	
Skull and Crossbones	Skull and Crossbones Symbol	
Atomic Whirl	Symbol of Chaos	Ichthys Symbol
Croatian Interlace		

➢ Visual Perception and Distortions

Visual Perception	Visual Agnosia	Vertigo
Ianothinopsia	Dysmorphopsia	
Micropsia	Microtelepsia	
Macropsia	Pelopsia	
Xanthopsia	Achromatopsia	

- ➢ Numbers and Number Systems
- o Numbers

Hundred	Thousand	
Million	Billion	Trillion
Quadrillion		

- o Number Systems

Unary	Binary	Ternary
Quaternary	Quinary	Senary
Septenary	Octal	Nonary
Decimal	Hexadecimal	

- o Tuples

Single	Double	Triple
Quadruple	Quintuple	

- ➢ Time

Early	Late	
Past	Future	
Time	Present-Time	Current-Time
Second	Minute	Hour
Week	Month	Year
Decade	Millennia	
Epoch	Aeon	

> ## Computer Data

Bit	Byte
Kilobyte	Megabyte
Gigabyte	Terabyte
Petabyte	Exabyte
Zettabyte	Yottabyte

LIGHTING

> ## Types of Lights

Spotlight	Floodlight	
Frontlight	Halfrear Lighting	Backlight
Rim Lights	Rim Lighting	Marquee
Strobe	Strobe Light	Stroboscope
Flickering Light	Bubble Light	
Dim	Dim Lighting	Dark Lighting
Bright	Ultrabright	Blinding Light
Crepuscular Rays	Godrays	Rays of Shimmering Light
Artificial Lighting	Natural Lighting	
Sunlight	Direct Sunlight	Sunshine Ray
Sunbeams	Sunshaft	
Moonbeams	Starlight	

Waning Light	Radiant Light	
Incandescent	Fluorescent	
CFL	CFL Light	
Candlelight	Torch	Torch Light
Northern Lights		
Tesla Coil	Electric Arc	
Glow Stick	Blacklight	
Laser	Laser Light Show	
Dye-Laser	Ion-Laser	Gas-Laser
Gobo	Gobo Light	
Halogen	Argon Flash	
Lantern	Schwarz Lantern	Coleman Lantern
Flare	Ember Light	
Edison Bulb		
Nightlight	Christmas Lights	
Optical Fiber	Electroluminescent Wire	
Electromagnetic Spectrum		
Infrared	Ultraviolet	UV
X-Ray	Lightspeed	
Nightclub		
Glowing Radioactivity	Nuclear Waste	Glowing Nuclear Waste

> Lamps and Tubes

Flash-Lamp	Flashtube

Incandescent Lamp	Fluorescent Lamp	
Plasma Globe	Plasma Lamp	Lava Lamp
Crackle Tube		
Halogen Lamp		
Neon Lamp	Xenon Lamp	Krypton Lamp
Argon Lamp		
Helium Lamp	Carbide Lamp	
Argand Lamp	Diya Lamp	Arc Lamp
Gas Lamp	Gas Mantle	Kerosene Lamp
Tilley Lamp	Oil Lamp	
Mercury-Vapor Lamp	Metal-Halide Lamp	Sodium-Vapor Lamp
Sulfur Lamp	Hollow-Cathode Lamp	Electrodeless Lamp
Nixie Tube	Rubens-Tube	
Vacuum Tube Lamp	Geissler Tube	Dekatron

> ## Types of Displays

7 Segment Display	Dot Matrix Display	Electroluminescent Display
CRT	Phosphor Display	Vacuum Fluorescent Display
LCD	LED	
OLED	AMOLED	
Plasma Display	Quantum Dot	Quantum Dot Display
Jumbotron		

> ## Lighting Styles and Techniques

Lighting   Illuminated   Illumination

Moody Lighting   Mood Lighting

Cinematic Lighting   Studio Lighting   Cove Lighting

Soft Lighting   Hard Lighting   Accent Lighting

Volumetric   Volumetric Lighting   Contre-Jour

Rembrandt Lighting   Split Lighting   Beautiful Lighting

Low-Key Lighting   High-Key Lighting

Downlighting   Uplighting

Under-Illumination   Over-Illumination

Veiling Flare   Caustic Lighting   Ethereal Lighting

Nightclub Lighting   DJ Lighting

Concert Lighting   Museum Lighting

Light Pollution

Epic Light

➤   Global Illumination

Global Illumination   Lumen Global Illumination

Screen Space Global Illumination

Ray Tracing Global Illumination

Photon-Mapping

➤   Shadows

Shadow   Shadows   Ray Traced Shadows

Drop Shadow

MATERIAL PROPERTIES

> ➤ Opacity

Opacity

Transparent   Translucent   Opaque

> ➤ Optics and Light Manipulation

Optics   Materiality

Scattering   Subsurface-Scattering

Ambient Occlusion   Opalescent

Polarization   Polarized

Solarization   Solarized

Iridescent   Dispersion

Chromatic   Prismatic

Glitter   Sparkly   Sparkles

Scintillating

> ➤ Luminescence

Glowing   Glowing Neon   Glow-In-The-Dark

Radiant   Cherenkov Radiation

Luminescence

Bioluminescence   Photoluminescence   Chemiluminescence

Cathodoluminescence   Electroluminescence   Radioluminescence

Fluorescence   Phosphorescence   Thermoluminescence

Crystalloluminescence Piezoluminescence   Electrochemiluminescence

Triboluminescence   Mechanoluminescence   Lyoluminescence

Candoluminescence   Fractoluminescence   Sonoluminescence

Translucidluminescence

➢ Chromism

Chromism   Piezochromism   Tribochromism

Metallochromism   Ionochromism   Goniochromism

Hydrochromism   Cryochromism

Radiochromism   Concentratochromism   Vapochromism

Solvatochromism   Solvatophotochromism

Thermochromism   Thermochromatic   Thermosolvatochromism

Photochromism   Photovoltachromism   Photoelectrochromism

Halochromism   Halosolvatochromism

Cathodochromism   Amorphochromism   Sorptiochromism

Electrochromism   Electromechanochromism

Magnetochromism   Mechanochromism

Biochromism   Bioelectrochromism

Chronochromism   Crystallochromism

Rigidichromism   Aggregachromism

➢ Reflection and Refraction

Rough   Matte

Glossy	Shiny	Polished
Reflection	Reflective	Retroreflective
Refraction	Refractive	Caustics
Glare		
Specular Highlights		
Shimmer	Shimmering	Glimmering

➢ Phase Transitions

Melting	Freezing
Vaporization	Condensation
Sublimation	Deposition
Ionization	Deionization

➢ Texture Maps

| Bump Map | Bump Mapped | Bump Mapping |
| Normal Map | Depth Map | Displacement Map |

➢ Softness and Hardness

Soft	Hard
Soft Body	Squishy
Solid	

➢ Thickness

| Thin | Thick |

➢ Physical Properties

Blobby	Blobs
Cracks	Cracked
Corroded	
Dirty	With Imperfections
Carbonated	Effervescent
Icy	Charred
Corrugated	Perforated
Hydrophobic	
Flowing	

➢ Other Material Properties

Anisotropy

MATERIALS

➢ Solids
o Wood and Paper

Wooden

Plywood	Particle-Board	Hardboard
Lumber	Planks	Wooden Planks
Cork	Sawdust	Nailed-Wood
Wood Veneer	Spalting	Petrified Wood
Oak-Wood	Maple-Wood	Acacia-Wood

Pine-Wood	Cherry-Wood	Birch-Wood
Cedar-Wood	Wood-Stain	Wooden Fence
Containerboard	Fiber-Reinforced Composite	
Cardboard	Paperboard	Corrugated Fiberboard
Cardstock	Paper	Construction Paper
Tracing Paper	Glassine	Post-It Note
Tissue Paper	Graph Paper	Kraft Paper
Tissue	Tissues	
Wove Paper	Ingres Paper	Lokta Paper
Washi	Wasli	Vellum
Papyrus	Ancient Egyptian Papyri	
Manuscript Paper	Medieval Parchment	
Wrapping Paper	Parchment	Parchment Paper
Toilet Paper	Paper Towel	
Manila Paper	Manila Folder	Envelope
Security Paper	Rolling Paper	Cotton Paper
Hemp Fiber	Hemp Paper	Cellulose
Plastic-Coated Paper	Tar Paper	
Greaseproof Paper	Seed Paper	

o   <u>Soils</u>

Soil	Dirt	Clay
Mud	Mud Brick	Dust
Sand	Gravel	Silt

Sandpaper	Podzol	Spodosol
Kaolinite		

- o Stone and Minerals

Stone	Cobblestone	Pebbles
Rock	Rocky	Bedrock
Sandstone	Basalt	Flint
Marble	Gypsum	Borax
Granite	Diorite	Andesite
Mineral		
Coal	Sulfur	Slag
Slate	Limestone	Sodalime
Quartzite	Travertine	Minium
Chert	Fulgurite	Geyserite
Carbon Fiber	Graphene	Carbon Nanotubes
Concrete	Hempcrete	Sidewalk
Asphalt	Road	Stone Tablet
Brick	Terracotta	Pottery
Ceramic	Enamel	Tile
Sheetrock	Plaster	Asbestos
Vermiculite	Perlite	Fossil

- o Metal

Metallic	Metal	Liquid Metal

Foil	Rusty	Tarnish
Pewter	Copper	Tin
Aluminum	Brushed Aluminum	
Bronze	Brass	Tarnished Brass
Iron	Wrought Iron	Damascus
Steel	Stainless Steel	Damascus Steel
Titanium	Anodized Titanium	Damascus Titanium
Silver	Sterling Silver	Sterling
Tarnished Silver		
Gold	Rose-Gold	Tarnished Gold
Platinum		
Chromium	Chrome	
Bismuth	Bismuth Crystals	
Liquid Bismuth	Melted Bismuth	
Mercury	Mercury Metal	
Molten Mercury	Molten Mercury Metal	
Gallium	Melted Gallium	
Indium	Melted Indium	
Magnesium	Zinc	
Lead	Tungsten	Cobalt
Zirconium	Cubic Zirconium	
Sodium	Potassium	Uranium
Constantan	Hepatizon	Nichrome
Iron Filings	Copper-Sulfate	Metal Foam

Solder	Metallic Fiber	Armature Wire
Chain	Chain-Link	
Barbwire		
Fence	Chicken Wire	Chain-Link Fence

- o <u>Glass and Crystal</u>

Glassy	Stained Glass	Stained Glass Windows
Seaglass	Obsidian	
Mirror	Mirrored	Hall of Mirrors
Fiberglass	Glass Fiber	
Glass and Crystals	Crystalline	Borax Crystals
Diamond	Herkimer Diamond	Amethyst
Quartz	Smoky Quartz	Milky Quartz
Rose Quartz	Rutilated Quartz	Sceptred Quartz
Ruby	Sapphire	Emerald
Pearl	Citrine	Fluorite
Lapis Lazuli	Onyx	Selenite
Jasper	Opal	Opalite
Topaz	Agate	Carnelian
Ametrine	Aventurine	
Talc	Talcum Powder	Tridymite
Moganite	Stibnite	Cristobalite
Marcasite	Calomel	Realgar
Cuprite	Aqeeq	Lechatelierite

Sphalerite	Orpiment	Prasiolite
Chrysoprase	Chalcedony	
Jewelry	Colloidal Crystal	

o   <u>Cloth</u>

Cloth	Cotton	Polyester
Twine	Cashmere	
Silk	Satin	
Denim	Khaki	
Leather	Felt	Felt Cloth
Linen	Velvet	Corduroy
Microfiber	Fibers	Memory Foam
Nylon	Polyamide	Spandex
Kevlar	Rayon	Lyocell
Cordura	Lurex	Nomex
Rolag	Roving	Lurex
Swanskin Cloth	Tansukh Cloth	
Jute Cloth	Barkcloth	
Quilt	Blanket	Pillow
Lint	Cushion	Pin Cushion
Rug	Carpet	
Persian Rug	Qom Rug	
Yarn	Knitted	Crochet
Cross Stich	Needle Point	Embroidery

Applique	Lace	Macrame
Patch	Sewing	Sewen
Weave	Weaving	Quilling
Net	Netting	
Spider Web		

- o <u>Plastic and Foam</u>

Plastic	Polyimide	
Shrink Wrap	Plastic Wrap	Cling Wrap
Polyurethane	Polyethylene	Polyvinyl
Polypropylene	Teflon	Melamine
Styrofoam	Foam	Bubble Wrap
PLA	Polylactic-Acid	
ABS	Acrylonitrile-Butadiene-Styrene	
PETG	Polyethylene-Terephthalate-Glycol	
TPE	Thermoplastic-Elastomer	
TPU	Thermoplastic-Polyurethane	
PVA	Polyvinyl-Alcohol	
ASA	Acrylonitrile-Styrene-Acrylate	
PMMA	Poly-Methyl-Methacrylate	

- o <u>Rubber</u>

Rubber	Latex	Nitrile

| Vinyl | Silicone | Linoleum |
| Arborite | Formica | Sandarac |

o   Gelatinous and Spongy

Gel	Aerogel	Softgel
Silica Gel	Ballistic Gel	Ballistic Foam
Gelatinous	Sponge	Spongy

o   Wax

| Wax | Wax Paper | Shellac |
| Carnauba Wax | Candelilla Wax | Paraffin Wax |

o   Ice and Snow

| Ice | Blue-Ice | Dry Ice |
| Snow | Snowflake | |

o   Hair and Fur

Hair	Hairy	
Short Hair	Long Hair	Flowing Hair
Straight Hair	Wavy Hair	Curly Hair
Hairstyle	Afro	Mohawk
Fur	Furry	
Fuzz	Fuzzy	
Feathers	Feathery	

Eyebrows   Unibrow

Beard   Mustache

Bear Fur   Cow Fur

Dust-Bunny

   o   <u>Other Solids</u>

Material

Amber   Ivory   Bone

Fibrin   Collagen

Inlay   Trash

Googly Eyes

Pellets   Filament

Celluloid

   ➤   <u>Liquids</u>

Liquid   Fluidity

Water   Liquid Crystal

Lava   Magma   Molten Rock

Molten   Varnish

Ferro Fluid   Motor Oil   Oil

Gasoline   Turpentine   Mineral Oil

Danish Oil   Linseed Oil   Tung Oil

Sea Foam   Emulsion

Lipid

- ➢ Non-Newtonian Fluids and Polymers
  - o Slime and Putty

Slime	Flubber
Putty	Poster Tack

  - o Tape and Adhesives

Tape	Scotch Tape	Clear Tape
Duct Tape	Packing Tape	Masking Tape
Kapton	Kapton Tape	Double-Sided Tape
Gaffer Tape	Twill Tape	Caution Tape
Adhesive	Glue	Double-Sided Glue
Epoxy	Paste	

  - o Other Non-Newtonian Fluids and Polymers

Non-Newtonian Fluid

Polymer	Orbeez	Oobleck
Play-Doh	Plastisol	

- ➢ Gasses and Vapors

Air

Gas	Gaseous	
Vapor	Vaporized	
Vapor Plume	Wafting Vapor	Accumulated Vapor

Aerosol

Aerosol Plume	Wafting Aerosol	Accumulated Aerosol
Clouds	Fog	Mist
Mist Plume	Wafting Mist	Accumulated Mist

> Powders and Particulates

Powder	Smoke	
Smoke Plume	Wafting Smoke	Accumulated Smoke
Particulate	Particulates	

> Plasma and Energy

Plasma	Energy	
High-Vibrational-Energy		Low-Vibrational-Energy
Electric	Electrical	Electricity
Fire	Fireball	
Flame	Flamethrower	
Burn	Inferno	Ember
Explosion	Firework	

MISCELLANEOUS

Floss		
Red Shift Render	Indigo-Render	
Amethyst-Deceiver	Indigo-Milk-Cap	
Manila		
Pythagoras Tree	Dorure Gliding	Mold
Eggcrate		
High-Pass	Low-Pass	
Medium	Binder	
Detelecine		
Flux	Fluxus	
Bare	Sphube	

OBJECTS

> Food and Consumables
o Fruits and Vegetables

Fruit	Vegetable	
Fig	Mango	Cauliflower

o <u>Meats, Cheeses, and Eggs</u>

Beef	Wagyu	Tallow
Pork	Bacon	
Cheese		
Egg	Egg Yolk	

o <u>Bread</u>

Bread	Made of Bread	Pretzel
Shortcrust-Pastry	Flaky-Pastry	Puff-Pastry
Choux-Pastry	Phyllo	

o <u>Nuts and Beans</u>

Beans	Peanut	Coconut

o <u>Dishes and Meals</u>

Pizza	Hotdog	
Pasta	Spaghetti	Fettuccine
Gnocchi	Marconi and Cheese	

o <u>Sauces, Spreads, and Oils</u>

Vegetable Oil	Olive Oil
Butter	Margarine
Peanut Butter	Jelly
Alfredo	

Sour Cream	Sauce	Pasta Sauce
Ketchup	Mustard	
Mayonnaise	Mayo	

    o   <u>Candy and Sweets</u>

Cake	Wedding Cake	Cake Decorating
Brownies		
Churros	Syrup	Maple Syrup
Cream	Whipped Cream	Ice Cream
Candy	Lollipop	Taffy
Cotton-Candy	Candy-Floss	
Gummy Candy	Gummies	
Chocolate	Caramel	
Marzipan	Gum Paste	Modeling Chocolate
Sprinkles	Nonpareils	
Fondant Icing	Royal Icing	
Honeycomb	Creme Brule	
Eclair	Cannoli	Fruit-Tart
Gumdrop	Gum	
Dessertwave		

    o   <u>Beverages</u>

Soda	Coffee	Tea
Wine	White-Wine	Red-Wine

Champagne

Corona   Corona-Phenomenon

- ○ <u>Other Food and Consumables</u>

Food	Macaroni	
Gelatin	Agar	
Edible Ink	Food Coloring	Food Dye
Deep-Fried	Molecular Gastronomy	
Tincture		
Toothpaste		

- ➤ <u>Microscopic Objects</u>

Atom	Fullerene	Nanoparticle
Cells	Cellular	
Mitochondria	Mitosis	
DNA	Bacteria	Enzyme

- ➤ <u>Digital Objects</u>

Computer	Display	
Camera	Lens	Film
Vinyl Record	CD	
DVD	Blu-Ray Disc	
Videocasette	LaserDisc	Capacitance Electronic Disc
Holographic Versatile Disc		

Transistor	Diode	
Wires	Cables	
Flux Capacitor		
Clock	Analog-Clock	Digital-Clock
Wristwatch		

> ## Toys

Toy		
Pinwheel	Slinky	Newtons-Cradle
Jigsaw	Puzzle	Tangram
Maze		
Stress Ball	Koosh Ball	Koosh
Beach-Ball	Ball Pit	Zorb
Rubik's Cube	Kinetic-Sand	
Cards	Dominoes	Marbles
Chess	Pogs	
Lego	Lego-Mindstorms	Lego-Mindstorms-NXT
Lincoln-Logs	Megablocks	
Etch-A-Sketch	Lite-Brite	

> ## Clothing

Uniform	Outfit	Wearable
Jeans		
Tuxedo	Polo	Fedora
Dress	Dressed	

Shoe	Shoes	Hat
Glasses	Wearing Glasses	
Sunglasses	Wearing Sunglasses	
Necktie	Bow Tie	Bowtie
Jumpsuit		

> ### Instruments

Instrument

Piano	Accordion	Saxophone

> ### Vehicles

Car	Airplane	
Blimp	Hot Air Balloon	Auto

> ### Badges, Patches, and Trophies

Badge	Heraldic Badge
Trophy	Gorget Patch

> ### Good Luck Charms

Charm	Good-Luck-Charm	
Horseshoe	Amulet	Dreamcatcher

> ### Ambiguous Objects

Object

Stuff	Things	Items
Trinket	Knickknack	Nick-Nack
Bauble	Curio	Tchotchke
Doodad	Blobject	

> Other Objects

Dichroic-Prism	Dispersive-Prism	
Seashell	Toilet	Bean-Bag
Cage	Cheese Grater	
Bracelet	Ribbons	Fingerprint
Bling	Tesla Valve	
Flag	Bench	Yardstick
Backdrop	Greenscreen	
Veins		
Bunsen Burner		
Needle	Screw	Nail
Paper Clips		
Band-Aid	Bandage	Gauze
Rubber Band	Rubber Band Ball	Silly Band
Balloon		
Soap	Lipstick	
Plume	Mat	Teapot

PERSPECTIVE

> ## Views

Top-View	Side-View	Satellite-View
Worms-Eye View	Aerial View	View From an Airplane
Closeup	Closeup-View	Extreme Closeup
Wide Shot	Epic Wide Shot	
Centered-Shot	Selfie	
First-Person	First-Person View	Field of View
Third-Person	Third-Person View	Product-View

> ## Angles

Low Angle	High Angle

> ## Perspective and Projections

Perspective	Perspective Projection	Panini Projection
Miniature Faking	Brenizer Method	
Forced Perspective	Aerial Perspective	
Isometric		
Orthographic	Multiview Projection	
Axonometric	Axonometric Projection	
Dimetric Projection	Trimetric Projection	
Parallel Projection	Oblique Projection	

Anamorphosis   Linear Perspective   Accelerated Perspective

One-Point Perspective Two-Point Perspective Three-Point Perspective

Curvilinear Perspective

Cylindrical Perspective

Reverse Perspective   Inverse Perspective   Inverted Perspective

Divergent Perspective

➤ Cutaway View and Cross-Sections

Cross-Section

Cutaway   Cutaway-View   Cutaway Drawing

Exploded-View   Exploded-View Drawing

RAINBOW OF MIDJOURNEY COLORS

Dark-Gray   Gray   Dark-White   White

Light-Black   Light-Gray   Black

Tan   Light-Brown   Beige

Dark-Brown   Brown   Vivid-Brown

Dark-Maroon   Maroon   Light-Maroon   Vivid-Maroon   Scarlet

Dark-Red   Light-Red   Red   Vivid-Red

Dark-Orange   Light-Orange Vivid-Orange   Orange

Dark-Yellow   Yellow   Light-Yellow   Vivid-Yellow

Chartreuse   Light-Lime   Vivid-Lime

Olive-Green	Dark-Lime	Light-Green	Lime
Dark-Green	Green	Vivid-Green	
Dark-Cyan	Aqua	Teal	Turquoise
Light-Cyan	Vivid-Cyan	Cyan	
Dark-Blue	Blue	Light-Blue	Azure
Vivid-Blue	Indigo		
Dark-Purple	Purple	Light-Purple	Vivid-Purple
Violet			
Dark-Magenta			
Magenta	Vivid-Magenta	Light-Magenta	
Fuchsia	Vivid-Pink		
Dark-Pink	Pink	Light-Pink	

SFX & SHADERS

➢ Reflections

Lumen Reflections   Ray Tracing Reflections

Screen Space Reflections

Diffraction Grading

Reflection in a Puddle   Water Reflection

➢ Blurs

Blur	Blurred	
Blurry	Blur Effect	Tilt Blur
Surface-Blur	Radial-Blur	Gaussian-Blur
Motion	Motion-Blur	Drifting
Field-Blur		

➢ Parallax

Parallax		
Anaglyph		
Multiscopy	Autostereoscopy	Stereoscopy

➢ Distortion

Distortion	Phase Distortion	
Barrel Distortion	Radial Distortion	
Amplitude Distortion	Harmonic Distortion	Frequency Response Distortion
Pincushion Distortion	Mustache Distortion	Group Delay Distortion
Morph	Morphing	
Interlace	Interlaced	
Lenticular	Continuous Droste	Tornadic

➢ Chromatic SFX

Chromatic Aberration	RGB Displacement	Spherical Aberration
Harris Shutter		

➤ <u>Stylized</u>

Color Banding

Scan Lines	Edge Detection	
Posterization	Quantization	
Sobel Operator	Convolution Matrix	
Moire Patterns	Twisted Rays	
Sabattier Effect	Quantum-Wavetracing	

Textured

Glowing Edges

Tessellated	Emboss	Starburst
Cropped	Sharpened	
Dilate	Erode	
Smudged	Mordancage	
Recursion	Repetition	

Tracers

Volume	Oscillation	

➤ <u>Shaders and Post Processing</u>

Ray Traced	RTX	Ray Tracing Ambient Occlusion
Shaders	OpenGL-Shaders	GLSL-Shaders
Anti-Aliasing	FXAA	TXAA
Sharpen	Spot-Healing	Digitally Enhanced
Post Processing	Post-Processing	Post-Production
Haze	Volumetric Haze	

Tone Mapping

VFX   SFX   CGI

SSAO   De-Noise

Flat Shading   Gouraud Shading   Phong Shading

Cel Shading   Gooch Shading

SONG LYRICS

You can use *song lyrics* as prompts and the AI Tool will create some illustrations of the words. You can give it a try using some of your favorite songs. Be aware that every lyric has a *copyright* to it. It belongs to the person who wrote the lyric. If you are creating the image for commercial purposes I would avoid using the lyrics from someone else. You can use your own lyrics or you can use the help of Chat GPT to create some new ones if you are not the poetry type ☺

STRUCTURAL MODIFICATION

> ➤ Spirals, Loops, and Helixes

Whirl   Spiraling   Spiral

Hyperbolic Spiral   Euler Spiral   Fermat's Spiral

Logarithmic Spiral   Doyle Spiral   Triskelion

Spiral of Theodorus Archimedean Spiral   Golden Spiral

Spiral Stairs   Spiral Staircase

Loop-De-Loop   Loopy

Helix	Double-Helix	
Twisted	Coiled	

> ### Curves and Waves

Wave	Wavy	
Curve	Bezier Curve	
Curvaceous	Curvilinear	Sinuous
Curlicue		
Ripple	Squiggly	
Dimpled	Incurved	Incurvate
Arched	Arciform	
Arrondi	Sigmoid	
Serpentine		

> ### Knots

Knot	Unknot
Entangled	Entanglement
Celtic Knot	Pretzel Knot

> ### Circular

Circle	Circular	
Rounded	Spherize	Spherical
Concentric	Concentric Circles	Concentric Rings
Concentric Spheres	Contour	

Circinate	Orbicular	Oblique

> ➤ Dull and Pointy

Pointy Pointed

> ➤ Other

Zig-Zag	Deflate	Inflate
Incline	Declinate	Biflected
Hollow	Enbowed	

TV SHOWS & MOVIES

When using movie titles think about the copyright and if you are not breaking some laws, which could lead to a potential lawsuit. It is always better to be more original and more creative. If you are in the search of a particular style, make a research regarding the style itself and describe it in your prompt rather than just using the title of the movie or the name of the director. Make research, and ask the community.

> ➤ Anime

Akira	Attack on Titan	Bakuman
Code Geass	Cowboy Bebop	Death Note
Detective Conan	Dr Stone	Dragon Ball Z
Fullmetal Alchemist	Gintama	Great Teacher Onizuka
Gurren Lagann	Haikyu	Hajime no Ippo

Hunter_x_Hunter   Inuyasha   Jojos Bizzare Adventures

Jujutsu Kaisen   Kimetsu no Yaiba (Demon Slayer)

Koe no Katachi   Vinland Saga

Mob Psycho 100   My Hero Academia   Naruto

Pokemon   Pokémon

One Piece   Ruroni Kenshin

Spirited Away   Steins Gate   Sword Art Online

Add your favorite shows:

_____

_____

_____

➤ TV Shows

TV Show

Teletubbies

Rick and Morty   Simpsons   Family Guy

Adventure Time   Star Trek

Add your favorite shows:

_____

_____

_____

➤ Movies

Movie

Fantasia

Tron   In The Style of Tron

Saw   Godzilla

Add your favorite movies:

_____

_____

_____

THEMES

> Realism/Abstraction

Realistic	Hyperrealistic	Hyper Real
Photorealistic	Photorealism	
Realism	Magic Realism	Fantastic Realism
Classical Realism	New Realism	Contemporary Realism
Surreal	Surrealism	Unrealistic
Non-Fiction	Fiction	Science Fiction
Imagined	Imaginative	Imagination
Dreamlike	Dreamy	Fever-Dream
Dreampunk	Daydreampunk	
Dreamcore	Weirdcore	
Worldly	Otherworldly	Unworldly
From Another Realm	Wonderland	

Lucid	Ethereal	Ethereality
Anemoiacore	Déjà vu	
Abstract	Abstraction	Lyrical Abstraction
Fantasy	Ethereal Fantasy	Dark Fantasy
Fantasy Map		
Illusion	Impossible	Nonsense
Immaterial	Intangible	
Visual Rhetoric	Visual Exaggeration	
Exaggerated	Exaggeration	

> ➢ Retro/Modern

Retro	Retrowave	
Nostalgiacore	Nostalgia	
Vintage	Antique	
Cyberpunk	Postcyberpunk	
Atompunk	Nanopunk	
Raypunk	Rollerwave	
Rustic	Rusticcore	Rococopunk
Pre-Historic	Historic	Prehistoricore
Jurassic	Ice Age	Wild West
Modern	Modernismo	
Futuristic	Futurism	Future Funk
Retro-Futurism	Cassette Futurism	Afrofuturist

> ➢ Sci-fi

Sci-fi	Alchemy	
Terrestrial	Extraterrestrial	Alien
Invaded	Invasion	
Aurora	Aurorae	Auroracore
Weirdcore Aurora		
Magic	Magical	Magicpunk
Spell		
Mystic	Mystical	
Psychic	Metaphysical	
UFO	Lightsaber	
Aetherpunk	Decopunk	
Dracopunk	Dragoncore	Unicorncore
Fairycore	Fairy Folk	Spriggancore
Angelcore	Supernatural	
Cryptidcore	Ghostcore	Spiritcore
Cypernoir	Goblincore	Rangercore
Witchcore	Wizardcore	Magewave
Mythpunk		
Eye of Providence		
Illuminati		

➢ Rooms

Room

Inside	Internal	
Outside	External	
Hotel Room	Apartment	
Labyrinth		
Living Room	Lounge	
Den	Front Room	
Dining Room	Kitchen	
Bedroom	Guest Room	Bathroom
Hallway	Passageway	
Greenhouse	Atrium	
Conservatory	Sun-Room	
Study	Library	
Office	Home-Office	
Attic	Crawlspace	
Basement	Cellar	Wine-Cellar
Rooftop	Underground	
Storage Room	Closet	
Laundry Room	Utility Room	Mud-Room
Garage	Shed	
Porch	Balcony	
Game Room	Home Theater	Gym Room
Nursery	Prayer Room	

> ## Architecture and Manufactured

Cityscape	Architecture	Balinese Architecture
Structure	Structural	Scaffolding
Manufactured	Makeshift	
Bronzepunk	Steelpunk	Clockpunk
Steampunk	Dieselpunk	Gadgetpunk
Funhouse	Toyland	Carnival
Salvagepunk	Silkpunk	Sandalpunk
Swordpunk	Cassettepunk	Formicapunk
Brutalism	Sphinx	Ziggurat
Industrial Design	Googie	
Pillar		
Shack	Property	Company
House	Multiplex	
Castle	Mansion	Kingdom
Playground	Poolcore	
Labcore	Nuclear	
Machine	Submachine	Machinescape
Robotic	Cyborgism	Autonomous
Legopunk	Legogearpunk	
Tinkercore	Craftcore	
Stimwave	Wormcore	
Barbiecore	Dollcore	Sanriocore
Palewave	Normcore	

Bombacore   Thriftcore

Dollpunk

> ### Music Styles

Music   Musical   Musical Notation

Musica

Funky   Groovy   Disco

Punk   Post-Punk   Folk Punk

Hip-Hop   Rave

Vaporwave   Synthwave   Chillwave

Hypnagogic Pop   Hyperpop   K-Pop

Tenwave   Bardcore   Breakcore

Cargopunk

Shpongle   In The Style of Shpongle

> ### Cartoons, Anime, and Comics

Cartoon   Marvel Comics

Anime   Animecore   Manga

Kawaii   UwU

Manhwa

> ### Colors, Crystals, Sparkles, and Light

Crystalcore   Sparklecore

Rainbowcore   Pastelwave   Pastelpunk

Glowwave   Glo-Fi   Neonpunk

Lightcore

Fractalpunk

Chromiesthesia

> ## Mood Based Themes

Warmcore   Lovecore

Happycore   Smilecore

Gloomcore   Dullcore

Dazecore   Sleepycore

> ## Other Themes

Dark Aesthetic

Gourmet

Archetype

Airborne

Microcosm   Macrocosm

Cleancore   Safetycore

Academia

Tinycore   Miniaturecore   Miniature World

Honeycore   Jamcore

Infinitywave   Infinitycore   Infinitypunk

MLG   Materialisimo   Slimepunk

Cyberpunk

Piwave   Fibonacciwave

Misterboombasicsuperfantasticwave

ARTISTS

➢ <u>Realism</u>

Painting By Ivan Shishkin   Painting By Zdzislaw Beksinski

Art by James Gurney   Painting By Claude Lorrain

Painting By Edward Hopper

Painted By Adolph Menzel   Painted By Alexei Savrasov

Painted By Andrew Wyeth   Painting By Vilhelm Hammershoi

➢ <u>Surrealism</u>

Painting By Salvador Dali   Painting By Pablo Picasso

Painted By Andre Masson

Painting By Max Ernst   Painting By Rene Magritte

Art By Jim Burns   Art by Vincent Di Fate

➢ <u>Idealism</u>

Painting By Jean Delville

➢ <u>Abstract</u>

Painting By Marcia Santore   Painting By Wassily Kandinsky

➤ Modernism

Painting By Kandinksey

Painting by Paul Cezane

Painted By Lawrence Pelton

Painted By Amanda Sage

Art by Henry Moore

Painted By Amedeo Modigliani

➤ Post-Impressionism

Painting By Van Gogh

➤ Art Nouveau

Painting By Wes Anderson

Painted By Alphonso Mucha

Painted By Gustav Klimt

➤ Luminism

Painting By Albert Bierstadt

Painting By Thomas Kinkade

➤ Expressionism

Painted By Affadi

Painted By Alexej Von Jawlensky

Painted By Alice Neel

Painted By Alyssa Monks

Painted By Alfred Kubin

➤ Futurism

Painting By David Alabo

- Gothic

Painted By Anne Stokes   Painting By Gerald Brom

Painting By Grant Wood   Painted By Albrecht Durer

- Psychedelic

Painting By Alex Grey   Painting By Dan Mumford

- Pop Art

Painted By Andy Warhol   Painting By David Hockney

- Concept Art

Painting By Marc Simonetti   Painted By Alan Lee

- Romanticism

Painting By John Constable

- Renaissance

Painted By Da Vinci   Painted By Leonardo Da Vinci

Painting By Hieronymus Bosch

- Vedute Painting Style

Painting By Canaletto

- Baroque

Painted By Annibale Carracci   Painted By Anthony Van Dyck

- ➤ Dadaism

Art By Man Ray   Painting By Robert Rauschenberg

Art By Marcel Duchamp

Painting By Morton Livingston Schamberg

Art By Suzanne Duchamp   Painting By Francis Picabia

Painting By Juliette Roche   Art By Georges Ribemont-Dessaignes

Art By Max Ernst   Art By Wilhelm Fick

Art By George Grosz   Art By Hannah Hoch

Art By Kurt Schwitters   Painting By Julius Evola

Art By Ilia Zdanevich   Painting By Serge Charchoune

Painting By Jean Crotti   Art By Sophie Taeuber-Arp

- ➤ Neo-Dadaism

Art By Genpei Akasegawa   Painting By Josip Demirovic Devj

Painting By Jim Dine   Art By Arthur Kopcke

Art By George Maciunas   Art By Valery Oisteanu

Painting By Ushio Shinohara   Art By Jean Tinguely

Art By Masunobu Yoshimura

- ➤ Instagram Artists

Uon.visuals   Art By Uon.visuals

Art By Seth McMahon

Artofethan   Art By Artofethan

Painting By Peter Mohrbacher

Painting By Boris Groh

- ➤ Artstation Artists

Painted By Annton Fadeev   Painted By Alena Aenami

Painted By Andreas Rocha   Painted By Aleksi Briclot

Painting By Ivan Stan

- ➤ Manga

Painting By Junji Ito

Painted By Akihiko Yoshida   Painted By Anton Pieck

Painted By Angus McKie   Painted By Akari Toriyama

Painted By Al Williamson

Art by Ilya Kuvshinov

- ➤ Non-Painters
- o Sculptors

Art By Alberto Giacometti   Art By Alexander Milne Calder

- o Photographers

Art By Anne Geddes   Art By Joel-Peter Witkin

o   Writers

Art By Anne McCaffrey

➤   Other Artists

Painting By Bob Ross	Art By M.C. Escher
Painting By Boris Smirnoff	Painted By Anton Otto
Painted By Ansel Adams	Painted By Alexander Jansson
Art By Ray Harryhausen	Art By H.R. Giger
Painted By Anna Dittmann	Painting By Raja Ravi Varma
Painting By Hugh Ferriss	Painted By Alexandre Cabanel
Painting By John Howe	Painted By Squidward Tentacles

NATURE & ANIMALS

➤   Biomes and Landscapes

Biome	Landscape	Surroundings
Setting	Settings	
Woodland	Forest	Rainforest
Coniferous Forest	Deciduous Forest	
Jungle	Junglecore	Tropical
Scrubland	Shrubland	Heathland
Thicket	Orchard	Chaparral

Park	Plains	Meadow
Grassland	Rangeland	Pasture
Prairie	Steppe	
Valley	Foothills	
Grove	Mangrove	
Swamp	Bayou	Bog
Marsh	Wetland	
Muskeg	Fen	
Tundra	Glacier	
Arctic	Polar	
Desert	Desertwave	Dunes
Savanna	Dryland	
Beach	Mediterranean	
Seaside	Sea	Deep Sea
Ocean	Ocean Grunge	Aquascape
Pond	Springs	
River	Lake	Waterfall
Coral Reef	Reefwave	Kelp Forest
Estuary	Floodplain	Hot Springs
Canyon	Mountains	Elevation
Crag	Cave	
Volcano	Volcanic	
Wasteland		

➤ Nature

Nature	Naturecore	Natural
Botanical		
Atmosphere	Environment	Ozone
Bloom	Bloomcore	Flowercore
Mosscore	Mushroomcore	
Earthcore	Organic	Lush
Garden	Japanese Garden	
Biopunk	Forestpunk	Groundcore
Icepunk	Frostpunk	Stonepunk
Creature	Frogcore	Paleocore
Crowcore	Ravencore	
Islandpunk	Seapunk	Selkiecore
Underwater	Nautical	Wetcore
Anthropomorphic	Nautical Nonsense	
Solarpunk	Lunarpunk	

➤ Plants

Plant	Plants	
Grass	Grassy	
Fern	Wheat	Aloe
Flowers	Floral	Vines
Tulip	Rose	Lilac
Dandelion	Daffodil	

Tree Bark	Branches	Leaves
Pinecone	Acorn	Sapling
Moss	Hemp	
Cactus	Bamboo	
Straw	Straw-Bale	
Hay	Hay-Bale	
Lily Pads	Water Lilies	
Kelp	Seaweed	
Tendrils		

> ## Fungi

Fungi	Mushroom	Mushrooms
Mycelium	Moldy	
Clathrus-Ruber	Amanita-Muscaria	Latticed-Stinkhorn
Entoloma-Hochstetteri	Cyptotrama-Asprata	Marasmius-Haematocephalus
Favolaschia-Calocera	Tremella-Fuciformis	Hygrocybe-Cantharellus
Tremella-Mesenterica	Golden-Scruffy-Collybia	
Cystoagaricus-Trisulphuratus		
Clavaria-Zollingeri	Chlorociboria	Mycena Acicula
Lactarius-Indigo	Laccaria-Amethystina	

> ## Animals

Animal	Animals	Mammal
Human	Humanoid	Humanoid-Forms

Dragon	Dinosaur	
Dog	Bulldog	Wolf
Cat	Calico	
Tiger	Leopard	Lion
Chihuahua	Corgi	Shih Tzu
Cow	Horse	Zebra
Deer	Fox	
Elephant	Giraffe	Kangaroo
Pig	Porcupine	
Sheep	Goat	Llama
Bear	Grizzly Bear	
Panda	Polar Bear	
Monkey	Gorilla	
Bird	Dove	Parrot
Crow	Eagle	Owl
Flamingo	Peacock	
Duck	Goose	Turkey
Guinea Pig	Capybara	
Rabbit	Squirrel	
Reptile	Snake	
Frog	Toad	
Fish	Penguin	
Pegasus	Minotaur	

> Insects

Worms	Earthworm	Sandworm
Caterpillar	Butterfly	
Ant	Bee	Grasshopper

> Sealife

Sealife	Jellyfish
Fish	Zebrafish
Whale	Shark
Turtle	
Clam	Oyster
Sea Anemone	Sea Urchin
Crinoid	
Fish-Eye	Blue-Pinkgill

> Corals

Coral

Madrepora-Oculata	Zoanthid	
Corynactis-Californica	Euphylliidae	
Corynactis-Annulata	Caulastraea-Furcata	
Ricordea	Acropora-Secale	
Corynactis	Favites-Halicora	Favites-Pentagona
Tubastraea-Faulkneri	Pseudodiploria-Strigosa	
Euphyllia-Ancora	Euphyllia-Divisa	Euphyllia-Glabrescens

➢ Seasons and Weather

Seasons	Spring	Summer
Autumn	Winter	
Weather	Weathercore	Overcast
Breeze	Wind	
Moonbow	Fogbow	
Rain	Downpour	
Sleet	Snow	Hail
Lightning	Lightning Bolt	
Lightningwave	Thunderbolt	
Hurricane	Tornado	Microburst
Storm	Stormy	
Sandstorm		
Heat	Heatwave	Eruption
Tsunami	Flood	Flooded
Frozen-in-Time Photograph		

➢ Time of Day

Morning	Midday	Day
Noon	Afternoon	
Dusk	Night	
Midnight	Twilight	Dawn

OUTER SPACE

> ➤ <u>Galaxies, Nebulae, and Other Cosmic Structures</u>

Galaxy

Nebula	Supernova	Hypernova
Vela Pulsar	Quasar	Microquasar

Asteroid

> ➤ <u>Black Holes and Singularities</u>

Blackhole	Wormhole

> ➤ <u>Planetary Bodies</u>

Planet	Planets	Planetary
Planet Mercury	Planet Venus	
Earth	Planet Earth	Global
Mars	Planet Mars	
Jupiter	Planet Jupiter	
Saturn	Planet Saturn	
Uranus	Planet Uranus	
Neptune	Planet Neptune	
Pluto	Planet Pluto	

- ➤ Stars

Sun

Starry   Stellar Corona

Neutron Star   Magnetar

Constellation

- ➤ Types of Matter

Antimatter   Dark Matter

- ➤ Solar Phenomena

Solar Eclipse   Eclipse

- ➤ Other

Spacecore   Cosmic   Celestial

Stellar   Interstellar   Interstellar Space

Galactic   Lunar

Outer Space   Universe

Orbital   NASA

Crab Pulsar

OTHER FREE AND PAID TOOLS

As it turns out there are many AI tools, some of them in Beta-versions, i.e. in the developing process, which you can use for free (for now), so you don't have to pay to practice your AI image generation. You can join them as easily as Midjourney, using Discord, and start generating. Some of them allow you to message the Bot directly! Wow, yes! This means you can have your own private channel, in which you can create your art undisturbed by other users. Another great side of this is that this way your ideas can stay hidden from others until you are ready to show or sell your art to the public. Always remember to do your own research on how much you have to pay to use these tools. Some tools are better than others, but all of them have a unique style that can be adapted according to your needs. And at the top of the list, you got *Blue Willow*! My favorite AI image generation tool, and yes, guys /imagine, it's free!

Here is a list of names and links to AI tools for which you can use this book:

Blue Willow	https://www.bluewillow.ai/
Stable Diffusion	https://stablediffusionweb.com/
StarryAI	https://starryai.com/
DALL-E 2	https://openai.com/dall-e-2/
Jasper Art	https://www.jasperai.com/art/
Nightcafe	https://nightcafe.studio/
Dream by Wombo	https://dream.ai/
Deep AI	https://deepai.org/
Deep Dream Generator	https://deepdreamgenerator.com/
Wonder	https://www.wonder-ai.com/
Artbreeder	https://www.artbreeder.com/
Stablecog	https://stablecog.com/
Fotor	https://www.fotor.com/
Runway ML	https://runwayml.com/
Big Sleep	https://github.com/lucidrains/big-sleep

EPILOGUE

Creating AI-generated art offers a wealth of benefits for both artists and art enthusiasts alike. Not only does it allow for an endless array of possibilities and creative expression, but it also provides a platform for artists to explore new avenues and push the boundaries of traditional art forms. With AI-generated art, people can create unique and stunning pieces, even with little knowledge, opening up a world of new opportunities and possibilities.

A great benefit of AI-generated art is its accessibility. It has made art-making accessible to anyone, regardless of their background or experience. Even if you've never picked up a paintbrush or pencil before, you can still create beautiful and unique art with just a few clicks of a button. This accessibility has also created a more diverse art community, with artists from all over the world sharing their unique styles and ideas.

AI-generated art has the ability to inspire and provoke thought. AI-generated art challenges our perceptions of what art is and what it can be, inspiring us to think outside the box and explore new ideas and concepts. It encourages us to question the relationship between technology and art and how they can work together to create something truly unique and beautiful.

Not to forget that creating AI-generated art can also be a profitable venture. With the rise of online marketplaces and stock photo websites, artists can now sell their art to a global audience, earning a living from their passion.

AI-generated art has the power to change the way we think about and create art. It offers endless possibilities, inspires creativity, and provides a platform for artists to share their work with the world. So give it a try and see where your AI-adventure takes you. You never know, you might just create something amazing!

If you enjoyed this book and found it helpful, please leave a **review** to help others to find it too. Thank you!

Notes:

_____

_____

_____

_____

_____

_____

_____

_____

_____

_____

_____

_____

_____

_____

_____

_____

_____

_____

_____

_____

_____

_____

_____

_____

_____

_____

_____

_____

Notes:

Printed in Great Britain
by Amazon

27670447R00066